Girl Saints
for Little Ones
Volume 2

Written by Kimberly Fries

Illustrated by Sue Kouma Johnson

Copyright © 2019 Kimberly Fries. All rights reserved.

www.mylittlenazareth.com

No part of this book may be reproduced by any means without the written permission of the author.

First Edition: April 2019

ISBN-13: 9781075092671

This book is dedicated to my daughters,
Maria Rose and Lily Marie, and Chiara Mary.
May these beautiful saints always guide and inspire you.

I shall do everything for heaven, my true home.
- St. Bernadette

St. Catherine
of Siena

St. Catherine was very devoted to her family. She liked to think that her father was like Jesus, her mother like Mary, and her brothers like the apostles. She loved Jesus so very much, that she desired to be his bride forever. In a vision, she was even given a ring by Jesus to show that they were married. She loved serving the poor and sick, and even helped the pope bring peace into the church.

Do not be satisfied with little things, because God wants great things! - St. Catherine of Siena

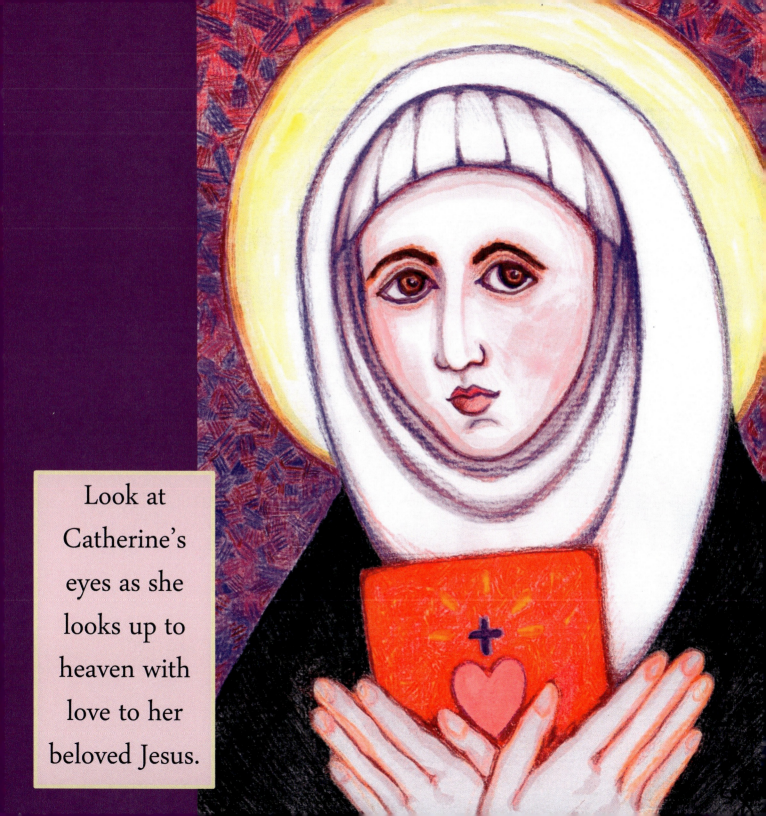

Look at Catherine's eyes as she looks up to heaven with love to her beloved Jesus.

St. Rose of Lima

Rose received the name Rose because everyone thought she looked as beautiful as a rose. She loved to sew, garden, and sell flowers. She also loved to pray and went to Mass and adoration every day. When she was twenty years old, Rose decided to become a Dominican, but still lived in a little house by her parents' house. She cared for poor children and the elderly that would visit her.

Apart from the cross, there is no other ladder by which we may get to heaven.

\- St. Rose of Lima

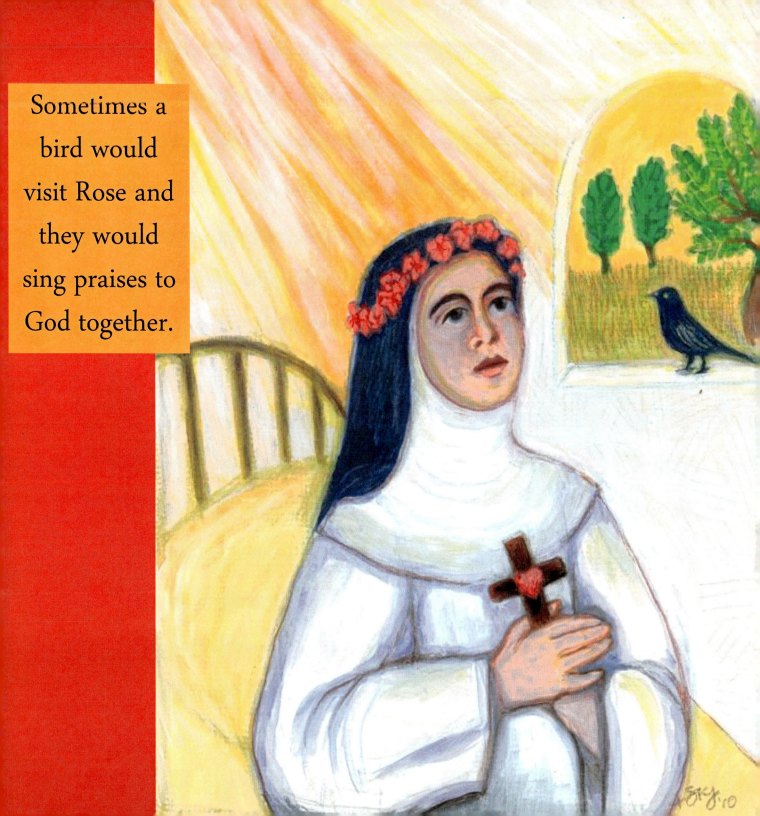

Sometimes a bird would visit Rose and they would sing praises to God together.

St. Elizabeth
of the Trinity

When Elizabeth was young, she was very smart and loved to play piano, but she also had a bad temper and was very stubborn. As she grew older and received her first Holy Communion, she began to feel very close to Christ and prayed often. By 14, she was convinced that she wanted to be a Carmelite nun. Though she died at only 26 years old, she grew to have such a great love of the Trinity!

It seems to me that I have found my Heaven on earth, since Heaven is God and God is in my soul. — St. Elizabeth

Elizabeth had a very deep prayer life, so a bright and beautiful spiritual world was open to her.

St. Rita

Though Rita wanted to be a nun since she was a young child, she was forced to marry. Her husband had a bad temper, but Rita helped him control it and love God more. However, one day he was killed and not long after her two sons died, too. Rita then became a nun. Before she died, she asked for a rose from her garden in her old home. Though it was the middle of winter, they found a rose and brought it to Rita.

Most Holy Sacred Heart of Jesus, help my heart to persevere in all that is holy. – St. Rita

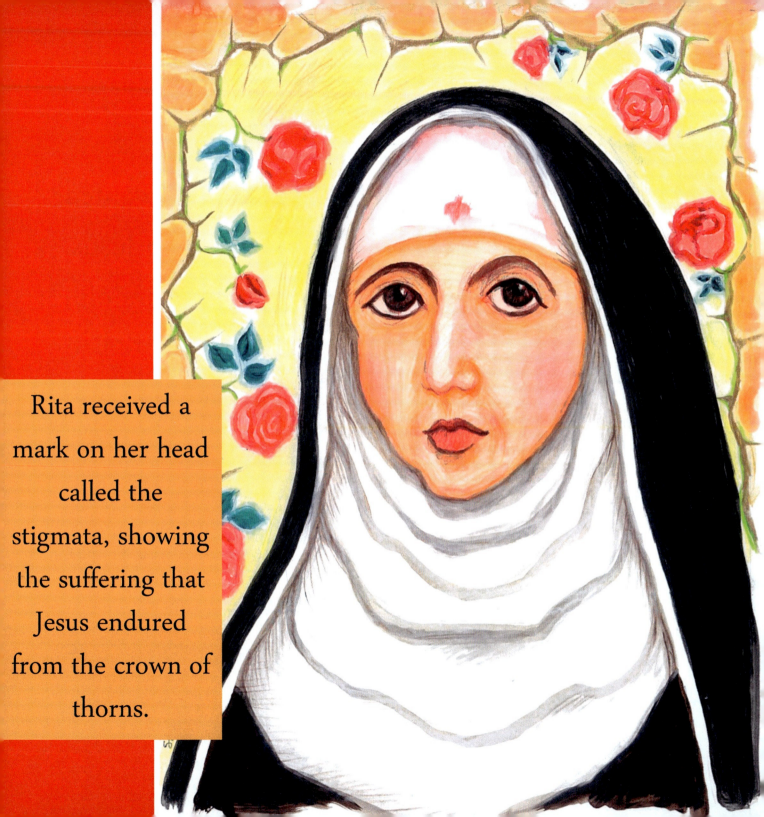

Rita received a mark on her head called the stigmata, showing the suffering that Jesus endured from the crown of thorns.

St. Agnes

Agnes was a very beautiful girl, who wanted only to become a nun and be married to Jesus. However, when she was only thirteen years old, there was a very powerful man who wanted to marry her. He said that she must deny God and marry him or else he would kill her. Little Agnes stood strong and wanted only to be with her beloved Jesus in heaven forever. She died for her faith and love of Jesus.

Christ has made my soul beautiful with the jewels of grace and virtue. I belong to Him Whom the Angels serve.

– St. Agnes

Agnes is holding a lamb because lambs are a symbol of purity.

St. Elizabeth

Elizabeth always wanted to have a baby, but was becoming very old. One day, an angel appeared to her husband, Zechariah, and told him that they were going to have a baby named John. When Elizabeth was pregnant with John, who was later called John the Baptism, her cousin Mary came to visit her. Since Mary was pregnant with Jesus, Elizabeth was filled with the Holy Spirit and baby John jumped in her womb.

Blessed are you who believed that what was spoken to you by the Lord would be fulfilled. – St. Elizabeth

Elizabeth is embracing her cousin, Mary, with open arms.

St. Perpetua
and St. Felicity

During the time Perpetua and Felicity lived, people were not allowed to say that they believed in God. When Perpetua, a young mother of a sweet baby boy, and Felicity, who was pregnant with a baby girl, decided to be Christians, they knew they would be martyred for their Faith in God. They knew that being a martyr was like having a golden ladder to heaven!

I cannot be called anything other than what I am, a Christian. - St. Perpetua

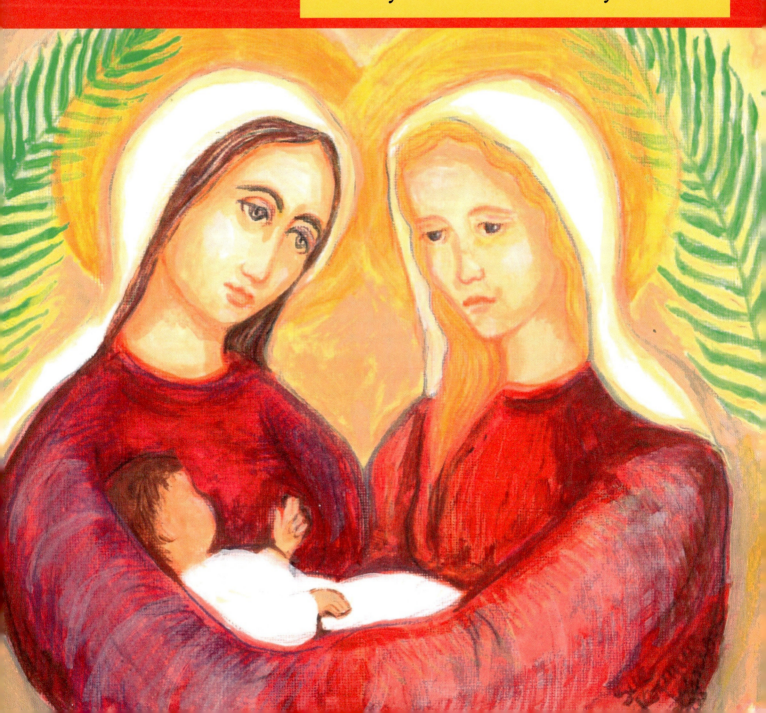

Perpetua and Felicity are wearing red to symbolize their martyrdom.

St. Zelie

Zelie married a wonderful and holy man, Louis, who also became a Saint. They had five daughters who all became Sisters, including St. Therese. Zelie enjoyed having her own business of making beautiful lace. She also was a wonderful mother whose greatest hope was for her children to became saints. She died of an illness when her children were still young, but she will spend all eternity with them.

Let us carry on bravely. – St. Zelie

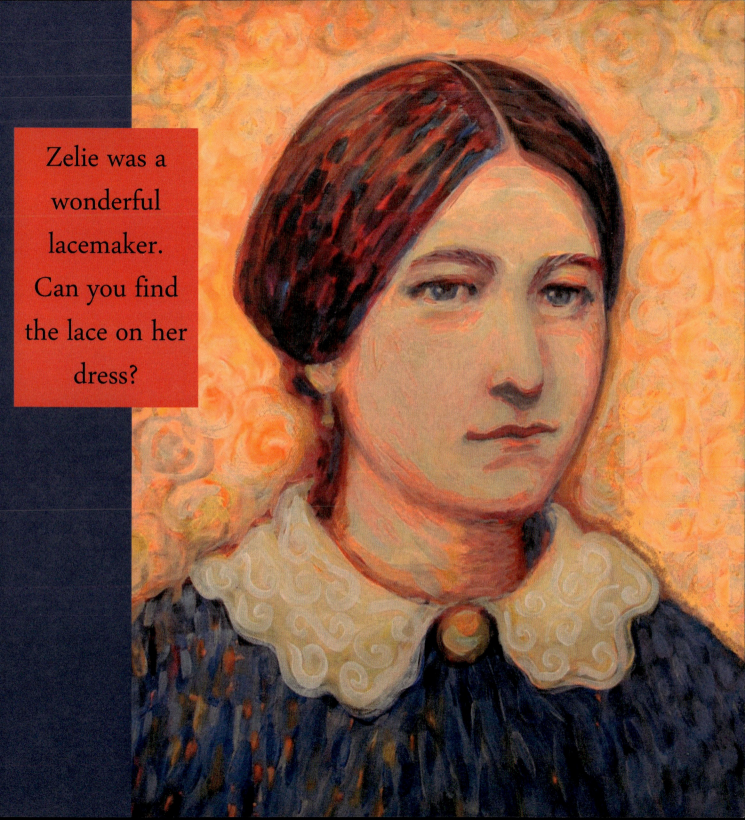

Zelie was a wonderful lacemaker. Can you find the lace on her dress?

St. Teresa of Avila

Teresa loved learning all about brave saints and martyrs with her brother when she was younger. When she grew up, she decided to become a Carmelite nun. She helped the Carmelites to live a more simple life focused on prayer. Teresa taught many people about how to have a life of prayer and relationship with God. She wrote many beautiful books.

I thought of the soul as resembling a castle, formed of a single diamond ... , and containing many rooms, just as in Heaven there are many mansions. — St. Teresa

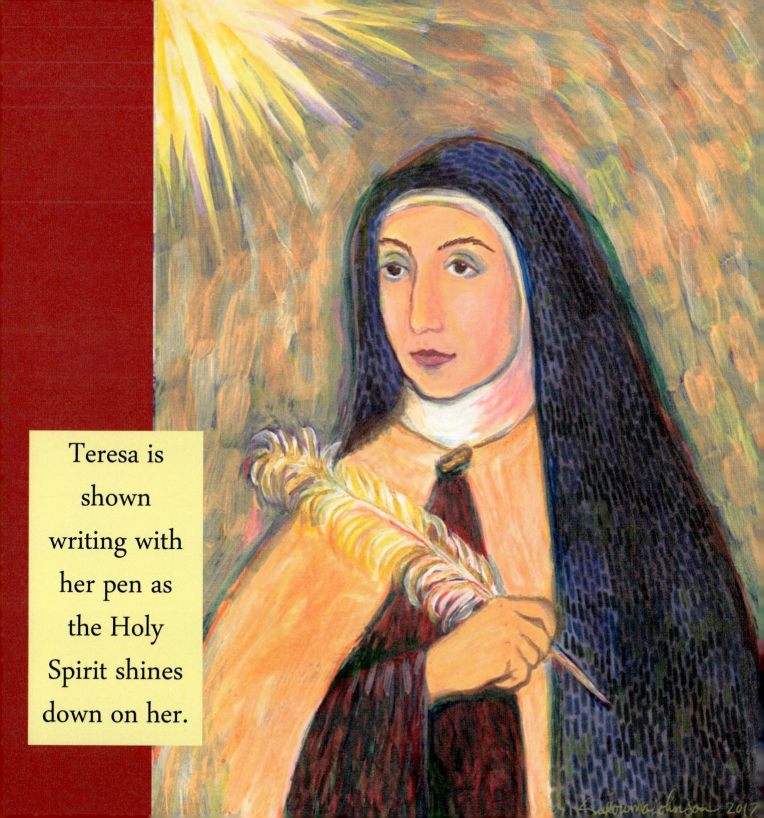

Teresa is shown writing with her pen as the Holy Spirit shines down on her.

St. Bernadette

Bernadette was very poor and suffered from asthma. Her family taught her to love God. One day, when Bernadette was 14, Mary appeared to her. Our Blessed Mother told her to drink water of the spring that appeared, which was miraculous water that could heal people. Mary also told Bernadette that she was the Immaculate Conception, meaning she was born without any sin on her soul.

I shall do everything for Heaven, my true home. There I shall find my Mother in all the splendor of her glory.
— St. Bernadette

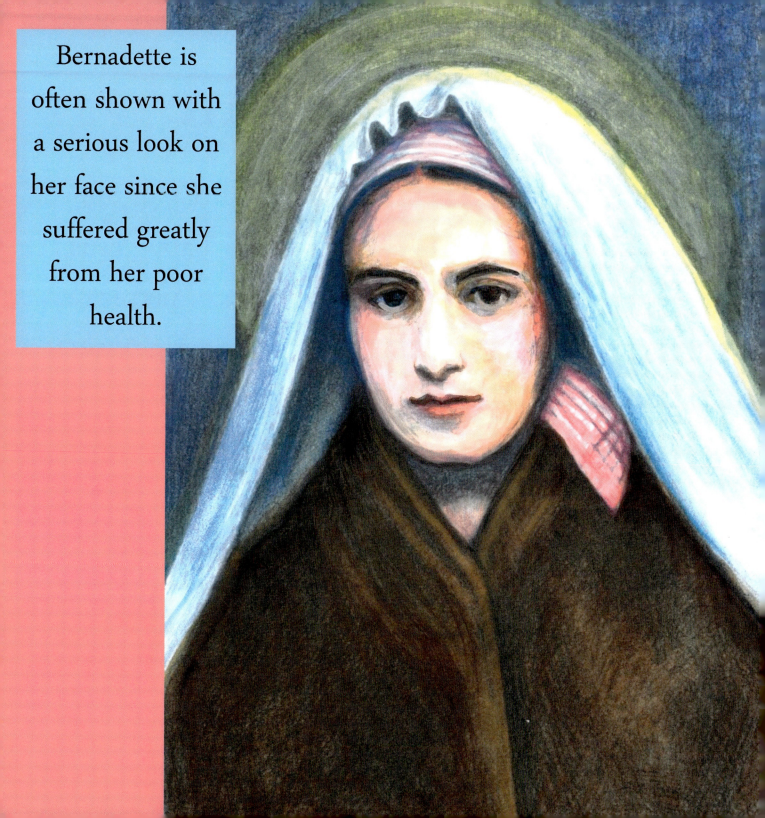

Bernadette is often shown with a serious look on her face since she suffered greatly from her poor health.

St. Catherine
of Alexandria

Catherine decided to become a Christian after seeing a vision of Mary and the baby Jesus. When the emperor decided to persecute Christians, he called upon Catherine and decided to ask her many questions about her faith. When everyone heard Catherine speak about God, many of them became Christians. The emperor did not like that, so Catherine was martyred.

Dear St. Catherine,

Please give me grace so that I may be brave and faithful.

Help me to love God like you love him!

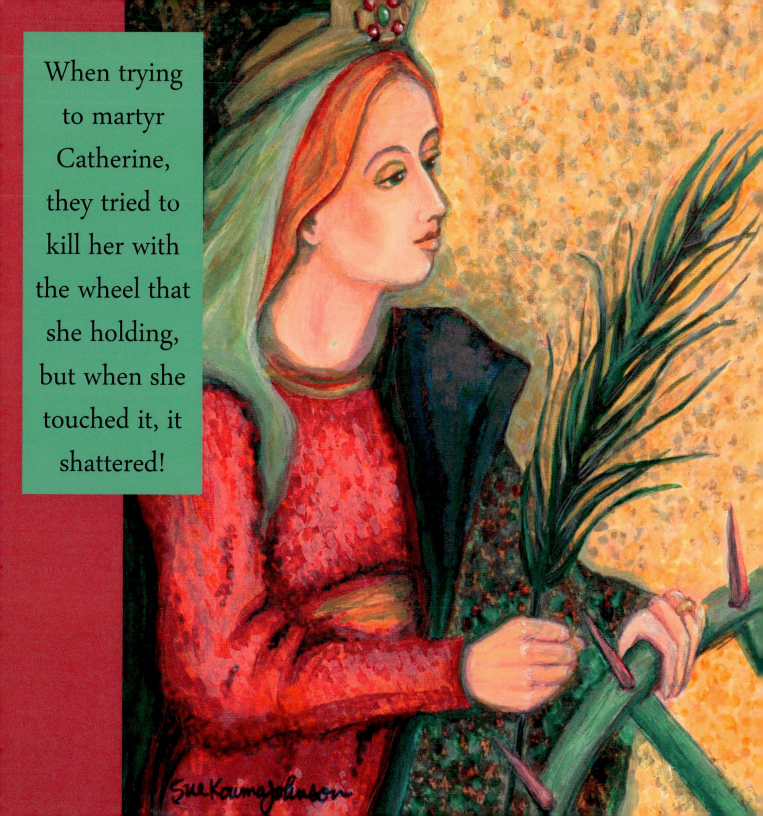

When trying to martyr Catherine, they tried to kill her with the wheel that she holding, but when she touched it, it shattered!

St. Gemma

Gemma always loved to pray. She really wanted to become a nun, but her health was too poor. Gemma thought about the sufferings of Jesus very often. She also had the stigmata, the wounds of Jesus, on her hands, feet, and heart. Sometimes she would be in such deep prayer that she would need to send her guardian angel to run errands for her. Eventually she died with a smile on her face, so happy to be with Jesus.

There is a school in heaven, and there one has only to learn to love. – St. Gemma

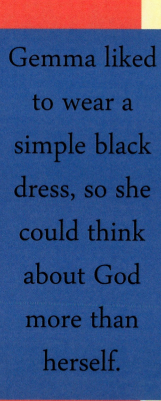

Gemma liked to wear a simple black dress, so she could think about God more than herself.

Collect them all!

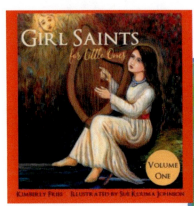
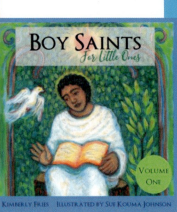
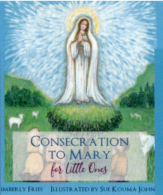

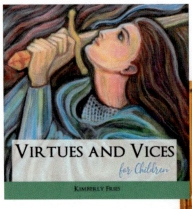
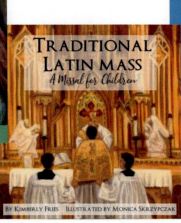
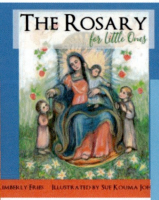
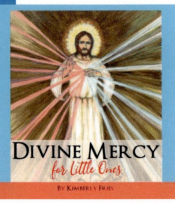

Bring Christ into your Home!

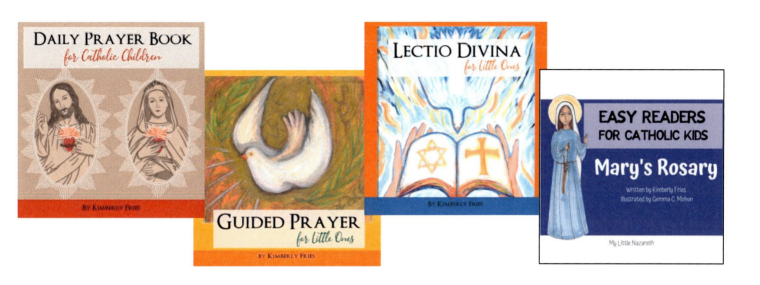
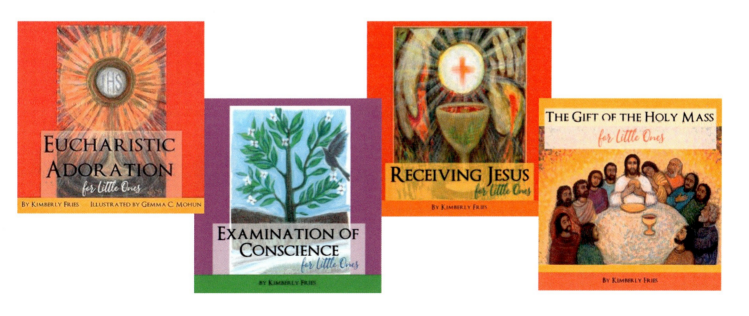

I would love to hear from you!

Please write a review at Amazon.com

Want to be the first to know about my new releases?
Follow me on Facebook, Instagram, Youtube, and my blog!
www.mylittlenazareth.com

Wholesale Prices also available!

Made in the USA
Las Vegas, NV
20 January 2025